La bohème

La bohème

Giuseppe Giacosa
and Luigi Illica

MINT EDITIONS

La bohème was first performed in 1896.

This edition published by Mint Editions 2020.

ISBN 9781513278247 | E-ISBN 9781513278704

Published by Mint Editions®

MINT EDITIONS

minteditionbooks.com

Publishing Director: Jennifer Newens
Design & Production: Rachel Lopez Metzger
Project Manager: Micaela Clark
Translated by W. Grist and P. Pinkerton
Typesetting: Westchester Publishing Services

Characters

Rudolph (a poet)	Tenor
Schaunard (a musician)	Baritone
Benoit (a landlord)	Bass
Mimi	Soprano
Parpignol	Tenor
Marcel (a painter)	Baritone
Colline (a philosopher)	Bass
Alcindoro (a councilor of state)	Bass
Musetta	Soprano
Custom-House Sergeant	Bass

Students, Work Girls, Citizens, Shopkeepers, Street Vendors, Soldiers, Restaurant Waiters, Boys, Girls, etc.

Time About 1830—In Paris

". . . Mimi was a charming girl specially apt to appeal to Rudolph, the poet and dreamer. Aged twenty-two, she was slight and graceful. Her face reminded one of some sketch of high-born beauty; its features had marvellous refinement.

"The hot, impetuous blood of youth coursed through her veins, giving a rosy hue to her clear complexion that had the white velvety bloom of the camellia.

"This frail beauty allured Rudolph. But what wholly served to enchant him were Mimi's tiny hands, that, despite her household duties, she contrived to keep whiter even than the Goddess of Ease."

Act I

In the Attic

Spacious window, from which one sees an expanse of snow-clad roofs. On left, a fireplace, a table, small cupboard, a little book-case, four chairs, a picture easel, a bed, a few books, many packs of cards, two candlesticks. Door in the middle, another on left.

Curtain rises quickly

RUDOLPH AND MARCEL: RUDOLPH *looks pensively out of the window.* MARCEL *works at his painting, "The Passage of the Red Sea," with hands nipped with cold, and warms them by blowing on them from time to time, often changing position on account of the frost.*

MAR.: (*seated, continuing to paint*) This Red Sea passage feels as damp and chill to me As if adown my back a stream were flowing.

(*Goes a little way back from the easel to look at the picture*)

But in revenge a Pharaoh will I drown.

(*Turning to his work*)

And you? (*to* RUDOLPH)

RUD.: (*pointing to the tireless stove*)

Lazily rising, see how the smoke
From thousands of chimneys floats upward!
And yet that stove of ours
No fuel seems to need, the idle rascal,
Content to live in ease, just like a lord!

MAR.: 'Tis now a good, long while since we paid his lawful wages.

RUD.: Of what use are the forests all white under the snow?

MAR.: Now Rudolph, let me tell you
A fact that overcomes me,
I'm simply frozen!

RUD.: (*approaching* MARCEL)

And I, Marcel, to be quite candid,
I've no faith in the sweat of my brow.

MAR.: All my fingers are frozen
Just as if they'd been touching that iceberg,

Touching that block of marble, the heart of false Musetta.

(*Heaves a long sigh, laying aside his palette and brushes, and ceases painting*)

RUD.: Ah! love's a stove consuming a deal of fuel!

MAR.: Too quickly.

RUD.: Where the man does the burning.

MAR.: And the woman the lighting.

RUD.: While the one turns to ashes.

MAR.: So the other stands and watches.

RUD.: Meanwhile, in here we're frozen.

MAR.: And we're dying of hunger.

RUD.: A fire must be lighted.

MAR.: (*seizing a chair and about to break it up*)
    I have it,
    This crazy chair shall save us!

(RUDOLPH *energetically resists* MARCEL'S *project*)

RUD.: (*joyous at an idea that has seized him*)
    Eureka!

(*Runs to the table and from below it lifts a bulky manuscript*)

MAR.: You've found it?

RUD.: Yes. When genius is roused ideas come fast in flashes.

MAR.: (*pointing to his picture*) Let's burn up the "Red Sea."

RUD.: No: think what a stench 'twould occasion!
    But my drama, my beautiful drama shall give us warmth.

MAR.: (*with comic terror*)
    Intend you to read it?
    Twill chill us!

RUD.: No. The paper in flame shall be burning,
    The soul to its heaven returning. (*with tragic emphasis*)
    Great loss! but the world yet must bear it,
    When Rome is in peril!

MAR.: Great soul!

RUD.: (*giving* MARCEL *a portion of the Ms.*)
    Here, take the first act.

MAR.: Well?

RUD.: Tear it.

MAR.: And light it.

(RUDOLPH *strikes a flint on steel, lights a candle, and goes to the stove with* MARCEL; *together they set fire to a part of the* Ms. *thrown into the fireplace; then both draw up their chairs and sit down, delightedly warming themselves*)

RUD.: How joyous the rays!

MAR.: How cheerful the blaze!

(*The door at the back opens violently, and* COLLINE *enters frozen and nipped up, stamping his feet, and throwing angrily on the table a bundle of books tied up in a handkerchief*)

COL.: Surely miracles apocalyptic are dawning!

For Christmas eve they honor by allowing no pawning!

(*Checks himself, seeing a fire in the stove*)

See I a fire here?

RUD.: (*to* COLLINE) Gently, it is my drama.

COL.: In blazes!

I find it very sparkling.

RUD.: Brilliant! (*the fire languishes*)

COL.: Too short its phrases.

RUD.: Brevity's deemed a treasure.

COL.: (*taking the chair from* RUDOLPH)

Your chair pray give me, author.

MAR.: These foolish entr'actes merely make us shiver.

Quickly!

RUD.: (*taking another portion of the* Ms.) Here is the next act.

MAR.: (*to* COLLINE) Hush! not a whisper.

(RUDOLPH *tears up the* Ms. *and throws it into the fireplace; the flames revive.* COLLINE *moves his chair nearer and warms his hands.* RUDOLPH *is standing near the two with the rest of the* Ms.)

COL.: How deep the thought is!

MAR.: Color how true!

RUD.: In that blue smoke my drama is dying

Full of its love-scenes ardent and new.

COL.: A leaf see crackle!

MAR.: Those were all the kisses.

RUD.: (*throwing the remaining* Ms. *on the fire*)

Three acts at once I desire to hear.

COL.: Only the daring can dream such visions.

RUD., MAR. AND COL.: Dreams that in flame soon disappear.

(*Applaud enthusiastically; the flame diminishes*)

MAR.: Ye gods! see the leaves well-nigh perished.

COL.: How vain is the drama we cherished.

MAR.: They crackle! they curl up! they die!

MAR. AND COL.: The author—down with him, we cry.

(*From the middle door two boys enter, carrying provisions and fuel; the three friends turn, and with a surprised cry, seize the provisions and place them on the table.* COLLINE *carries the wood to the fireplace*)

RUD.: Fuel!

MAR.: Wine, too!

COL.: Cigars!

RUD.: Fuel!

MAR.: Bordeaux!

RUD., MAR. AND COL.: The abundance of a feast day We are destined yet to know.

(*Exeunt the two boys*)

(*Enter* SCHAUNARD)

SCH.: (*triumphantly throwing some coins on the ground*)
    Such wealth in the balance
    Outweighs the Bank of France.

COL.: (*assisting* RUDOLPH *and* MARCEL *to pick up the coins*)
    Then, take them—then, take them.

MAR.: (*incredulously*) Tin medals? Inspect them.

SCH.: (*showing one to* MARCEL)
    You're deaf then, or blear-eyed?
    What face do they show?

RUD.: (*bowing*)
    King Louis Philippe: to my monarch I bow.

RUD., MAR., SCH. AND COL.: Shall King Louis Philippe at our feet thus lie low?

(SCHAUNARD *will go on recounting his good luck, but the others continue to arrange everything on the table*)

SCH.: Now I'll explain.
    This gold has—or rather silver—
    Has its own noble story.

MAR.: First the stove to replenish.

COL.: So much cold has he suffered,

SCH.: 'Twas an Englishman, then—
    Lord, or mi-lord, as may be—
    Desired a musician.

MAR.: (*throwing* COLLINE's *books from the table*)
    Off! Let us furnish the table.

SCH.: I flew to him.

RUD.: Where is the food?

COL.: There.

MAR.: Here.

SCH.: I pay my homage.

Accepted, I enquire—

COL.: (*preparing the viands on the table while* RUDOLPH *lights the other candle*)

Here's cold roast beef.

MAR.: And savory patty.

SCH.: When shall we start the lessons?

When I seek him, in answer to my question,

"When shall we start the lessons?"

He tells me "Now—at once.

Just look there,"

Showing a parrot on the first floor, hung, then continues:

"You must play until that bird has ceased to live."

Thus it befell:

Three days I play and yell.

RUD.: Brilliantly lightens the room into splendor.

MAR.: Here are the candles.

COL.: What lovely pastry!

SCH.: Then on the servant girl Try all the charms wherewith I'm laden;

I fascinate the maiden.

MAR.: With no tablecloth eat we—

RUD.: (*taking a paper from his pocket*) An idea!

COL. AND MAR.: The Constitutional.

RUD.: (*unfolding the paper*)

Excellent paper!

One eats a meal and swallows news at the same time!

SCH.: With parsley I approach the bird,

His beak Lorito opens;

Lorito's wings outspread,

Lorito opens his beak,

A little piece of parsley gulps—

As Socrates, is dead!

(SCHAUNARD, *seeing that no one is paying any attention to him, seizes* COLLINE *as he passes with a plate*)

COL.: Who?

SCH.: (*pettishly*) The devil fly away with you entirely!

(*seeing the rest in the act of eating the cold pastry*)

What are you doing?

(*With solemn gesture, extending his hand over the pastry*)
No! dainties of this kind
Are but the stored-up fodder
Saved for the morrow,
Fraught with gloom and sorrow, (*clearing the table*)
To dine at home on the day of Christmas vigil,
While the Quartier Latin embellishes
Its ways with dainty food and tempting relishes.
Meanwhile the smell of savory fritters
The old street fills with fragrant odor.
There singing joyously, merry maidens hover,
Having for echo each a student lover.

(RUDOLPH *locks the door; then all go to the table and pour out wine*)

RUD., MAR. AND COL.: 'Tis the gladsome Christmas Eve.

SCH.: A little of religion, comrades, I pray;
Within doors drink we, but we dine away.

(*Two knocks are heard at the door*)

BEN.: (*from without*) 'Tis I.

MAR.: Who is there?

BEN.: 'Tis Benoit.

MAR.: 'Tis the landlord is knocking!

SCH.: Bolt the door quickly!

COL.: (*calling towards the door*) No! There is no one!

SCH.: 'Tis fastened!

BEN.: Give me a word, pray!

SCH.: (*opening the door, after consulting with his friends*) At once.

BEN.: (*entering smilingly, showing a paper to* MARCEL) The rent!

MAR.: (*with great cordiality*) Hallo! give him a seat, friends!

BEN.: Do not trouble, I beg you.

SCH.: (*with gentle firmness, obliging* BENOIT *to sit down*) Sit down!

MAR.: (*offering* BENOIT *a glass of wine*) Some Bordeaux?

RUD.: Your health!

BEN.: Thank you.

COL.: Your health!

SCH.: Drink up!

RUD.: Good health! (*all drink*)

BEN.: (*to* MARCEL, *putting down his glass and showing his paper*) 'Tis the quarter's rent I call for.

Mar.: (*ingenuously*) Glad to hear it.

Ben.: And therefore—

Sch.: (*interrupting*) Another tipple? (*fills up the glasses*)

Ben.: Thank you.

Rud.: Your health!

Col.: Your health!

Rud., Mar., Sch. and Col.: (*all touching* Benoit's *glass*)
    Drink we all your health, sir! (*all drink*)

Ben.: (*resuming, to* Marcel)
    To you I come, as the quarter now is ended;
    You have promised,

Mar.: To keep it I intended. (*Shows* Benoit *the money on the table*)

Rud.: (*aside to* Marcel) Art mad?

Sch.: (*aside to* Marcel) What do you—

Mar.: (*to* Benoit, *without noticing the two*)
    Hast seen it? Then give your care a respite,
    And join our friendly circle.
    Tell me how many years
    Boast you of, my dear sir?

Ben.: My years! Spare me, I pray.

Rud.: Our own age, less or more?

Ben.: (*protesting*) Much more, very much more.

(*While they make* Benoit *talk, they fill up his glass immediately it is empty*)

Col.: He says 'tis less or more.

Mar.: (*mischievously, in a low voice*)
    T'other evening at Mabille
    I caught him in a passage of love.

Ben.: (*uneasily*) Me!

Mar.: At Mabille. T'other evening
    I caught you. Deny?

Ben.: By chance 'twas.

Mar.: (*in a flattering tone*) She was lovely!

Ben.: (*half drunk, suddenly*) Ah! very.

Sch.: Old rascal!

Rud.: Old rascal!

Col.: Vile seducer!

Sch.: Old rascal!

Mar.: He's an oak tree. He's a cannon.

Rud.: He has good taste, then?

BEN.: (*laughing*) Ha, ha!

MAR.: Her hair was curly auburn.

COL.: Old knave!

MAR.: With ardent speed leaped he joyous to her embraces.

BEN.: (*with increasing exultation*) Old am I, but robust yet.

RUD., SCH. AND COL.: Ardent with joy he sprang to her embraces.

MAR.: To him she yields her woman's love and truth.

BEN.: (*in a very confidential tone*)
  Bashful was I in youth,
  Now somewhat am I altered.
  Well, what I like myself. . .
  Must know that my one delight. . .
  Is a merry damsel,—and small,
  I do not ask a whale, nor a world-map to study,
  Nor, like a full moon,
  A face round and ruddy;
  But leanness, downright leanness, No! No!
  Lean women's claws oftentimes are scratchy,
  Their temper somewhat catchy,
  Full of aches, too, and mourning,
  As my wife is my warning.

(MARCEL *bangs his fist down on the table and rises; the others follow his example,* BENOIT *looking on in bewilderment*)

MAR.: A wife possessing!
  Yet thoughts impure confessing.

SCH. AND COL.: Foul shame!

RUD.: His vile pollution empoisons our honest abode.

SCH. AND COL.: Hence!

MAR.: With perfume we must fumigate!

COL.: Drive him forth, the reprobate!

SCH.: Morality offended hence expels you!

(BENOIT *staggeringly rises, and tries in vain to speak*)

BEN.: But say—I say!

MAR.: Be silent!

COL.: Be silent!

RUD.: Be silent!

(*They surround* BENOIT *and gradually push him to the door*)

BEN.: Sirs, I beg you!

MAR., SCH. AND COL.: Be silent, out, your lordship! Hence away!

GIUSEPPE GIACOSA AND LUIGI ILLICA

Rud., Mar., Sch. and Col.: Wish we your lordship a pleasant
    Christmas Eve. Ah!

(*They push* Benoit *outside the door*)

Mar.: (*locking the door*) I have paid the last quarter!

Sch.: In the Quartier Latin
    Momus awaits!

Mar.: Long live the spender!

Sch.: We'll the booty divide!

Rud.: We'll divide!

Col.: We'll divide! (*they divide the money on the table*)

Mar.: (*holding out a cracked mirror to* Colline)
    Beauty is a gift heaven descended,
    Now you are rich, to decency pay tribute.
    Bear! have your mane attended!

Col.: The first chance I can find,
    I will make acquaintance with a beard eraser!
    So guide me to the monstrous outrage of a barber's weapon.
    Let's go!

Sch.: We go!

Mar. and Col.: We go!

Rud.: I stay here, finish I must the article for my new journal,
    "Beaver"!

Mar.: Be quick then!

Rud.: Five minutes only, I know well the work!

Col.: We'll await you at the porter's lodge!

Mar.: Delay, and you'll hear the chorus!

Rud.: Five minutes only!

Sch.: You must cut short the Beaver's growing tale!

(Rudolph *takes a light from the table and goes to open the door: the others
go out and descend the staircase*)

Mar.: (*from without*) Look to the staircase! keep well to the handrail!

Rud.: (*on the landing near the open door holding up the candle*) Go
    slowly!

Col.: How plaguing dark 'tis!

Sch.: May the porter be damned!

(*The noise of someone falling is heard*)

Col.: I have tumbled!

Rud.: Colline, are you dead yet?

Col.: (*from the bottom of the staircase*) Not this time!

Mar.: Come quickly!

(Rudolph *shuts the door, puts down the light, clears a space at the table for pens and paper, then sits down and commences to write, after putting out the other candle*)

Rud.: I'm out of humor! (*A timid knock is heard at the door*) Who's there?

Mimi: (*from without*) Pardon!

Rud.: 'Tis a lady!

Mimi: Excuse me, my candle's gone out!

Rud.: (*running to open the door*) Is it?

Mimi: (*standing on the threshold with an extinguished candle and a key*) Pray, would you—

Rud.: Pray be seated a moment.

Mimi: No, I thank you.

Rud.: I beg you enter.

(Mimi *enters, but is seized with a fit of coughing*)

Rud.: Are you not well?

Mimi: No! Nothing!

Rud.: You are quite pale!

Mimi: (*coughing*) My breath—'tis the staircase—

(*Swoons, and* Rudolph *has hardly time to support her and place her on a chair. She lets fall her candlestick and key*)

Rud.: What can I do to aid her?

(*Fetches some water, and sprinkles her face*)

Ah! this! How very pale her face is! (*Mimi revives*) Do you feel better?

Mimi: Yes.

Rud.: Here 'tis very chilly.

Nearer the fire be seated an instant.

(*conducting her to a chair near the tire*)

A little wine?

Mimi: Thank you.

Rud.: (*giving her a glass and pouring out some wine*) For you.

Mimi: Not so much, please!

Rud.: Like this?

Mimi: Thank you. (*she drinks*)

Rud.: How lovely a maiden.

Mimi: Now please allow me to light my candle, I'm feeling much better.

Rud.: What, so quickly?

(Rudolph *lights the candle and gives it to* Mimi)

Mimi: Thank you. Now, good evening.

Rud.: So, good evening.

(*Accompanies her to the door, and then returns quickly to his work*)

Mimi: (*re-entering, stops on the threshold*)

Oh! how stupid! How stupid!

The key of my poor chamber,

Where can I have left it?

Rud.: Come, stand not in the doorway:

Your candle is flickering in the wind.

(*Mimi's light goes out*)

Mimi: Good gracious! Please light it just once more!

(Rudolph *runs with his candle, but, as he nears the door, his light, too, is blown out, and the room remains in darkness*)

Rud.: Oh, dear! Now there's mine gone out, too!

Mimi: Ah! and the key—where can it be?

(*Groping about, she reaches the table and deposits the candlestick*)

Rud.: What a nuisance! (*He finds himself near the door and fastens it*)

Mimi: I'm so sorry.

Rud.: Where can it be?

Mimi: You have an importunate neighbor, Pray, forgive your tiresome little neighbor.

Rud.: Nothing, I assure you.

Mimi: Pray, forgive your tiresome neighbor.

Rud.: Do not mention it, I pray you.

Mimi: Look for it.

Rud.: I'm looking.

(*Looks for the key on the floor; sliding over it, he knocks against the table, deposits his candlestick, and searches for the key with his hands on the floor*)

Mimi: Where can it be?

(*Finds the key, lets an exclamation escape, then checks himself and puts the key in his pocket*)

Rud.: Ah!

Mimi: Have you found it?

Rud.: No.

Mimi: I think so.

Rud.: In very truth.

MIMI: Found it?

RUD.: Not yet.

(*Feigns to search, but guided by Mimi's voice and movements, approaches her; as Mimi is stooping his hand meets hers, which he clasps*)

MIMI: (*rising to her feet, surprised*) Ah!

RUD.: (*holding Mimi's hand, with emotion*)

> Your tiny hand is frozen,
> Let me warm it into life;
> Our search is useless,
> In darkness all is hidden,
> 'Ere long the light of the moon shall aid us,
> Yes, in the moonlight our search let us resume.
> One moment, pretty maiden,
> While I tell you in a trice,
> Who I am, what I do,
> And how I live. Shall I?

(*Mimi is silent*)

> I am, I am a poet!
> What's my employment? Writing.
> Is that a living? Hardly.
> I've wit though wealth be wanting,
> Ladies of rank and fashion
> All inspire me with passion;
> In dreams and fond illusions,
> Or castles in the air,
> Richer is none on earth than I.
> Bright eyes as yours, believe me,
> Steal my priceless jewels,
> In fancy's store-house cherished,
> Your roguish eyes have robbed me,
> Of all my dreams bereft me,
> Dreams that are fair, yet fleeting.
> Fled are my truant fancies,
> Regrets I do not cherish,
> For now life's rosy morn is breaking,
> Now golden love is waking.
> Now that I've told my story,
> Pray tell me yours, too;
> Tell me frankly, who are you?

Say, will you tell?

MIMI: (*after some hesitation*)
    They call me Mimi
    But my name is Lucia;
    My story is a short one—
    Fine satin stuffs or silk
    I deftly embroider;
    I am content and happy;
    The rose and lily I make for pastime.
    These flowers give me pleasure
    As in magical accents
    They speak to me of love,
    Of beauteous springtime.
    Of fancies and of visions bright they tell me,
    Such as poets, and only poets, know.
    Do you hear me?

RUD.: Yes!

MIMI: They call me Mimi,
    But I know not why;
    All by myself I take my frugal supper,
    To Mass not oft repairing,
    Yet oft I pray to God.
    In my room live I lonely,
    Up at the top there, in my little chamber
    Above the house tops so lofty.
    Yet the glad sun first greets me;
    After the frost is over
    Spring's first, sweet, fragrant kiss is mine,
    Her first bright sunbeam is mine,
    A rose as her petals are opening
    Do I tenderly cherish. Ah! what a charm
    Lies for me in her fragrance!
    Alas! those flowers I make,
    The flowers I fashion, alas! they have no perfume!
    More than just this I cannot find to tell you,
    I'm a tiresome neighbor that at an awkward moment
    intrudes upon you.

SCH.: (*from below*) Eh! Rudolph!

COL.: Rudolph!

MAR.: Hallo! you hear not?

Don't dawdle!

(*At the shouts of his friends* RUDOLPH *is annoyed*)

COL.: Poetaster, come!

SCH.: What has happened, idler?

(*Getting more annoyed* RUDOLPH *opens the window to answer his friends; the moonlight enters, brightening the room*)

RUD.: I have still three lines to finish.

MIMI: (*approaching the window*) Who are they?

RUD.: My friends.

SCH.: You will know they're yours.

MAR.: What do you there, so lonely?

RUD.: I'm not lonely. We are two.

So to Momus go on.

There keep us places; we will follow quickly.

(*Remains still at the window to make sure of his friends going*)

MAR., SCH. AND COL.: (*gradually departing*)

Momus, Momus, Momus!

Gently and soft to supper let us go.

MAR.: And poetry let flow.

SCH. AND COL.: Momus, Momus, Momus!

(MIMI *goes nearer the window, so that the moon's rays fall on her while* RUDOLPH *contemplates her ecstatically*)

RUD.: Lovely maid in the moonlight!

MAR.: And poetry let flow.

RUD.: Your face entrancing.

Like radiant seraph from on high appears!

The dream that I would ever, ever dream, returns.

RUD.	MIMI.
	Love alone o'er hearts has sway
Heart to heart and soul to soul	Ah Love! to thee do we surrender.
Love binds us in his fetters.	(*yielding to her lover's embrace*)
(*placing his arm around* MIMI	
Love now shall rule our hearts alone,	Sweet to my soul the magic voice Of love its music chanteth,
Life's fairest flower is love!	Life's fairest flower is love!
Life's fairest flower is love!	(RUDOLPH *kisses her*)

MIMI: (*disengaging herself*) No, I pray you!

RUD.: My sweetheart!

MIMI: Your comrades await you!

RUD.: Do you then dismiss me?

MIMI: I should like—no, I dare not!

RUD.: Say!

MIMI: (*coquettishly*) Could I not come with you?

RUD.: What, Mimi?

    It would be much more pleasant here to stay.

    Outside 'tis chilly!

MIMI: To you I'll be neighbor! I'll be always near you.

RUD.: On returning?

MIMI: (*archly*) Who knows, sir?

RUD.: Take my arm, my little maiden!

MIMI: (*giving her arm to* RUDOLPH) I obey you, my lord!

(*They go, arm in arm, to the door*)

RUD.: You love me? Say!

MIMI: (*with abandon*)

    I love thee!

RUD. AND MIMI: My love! My love!

". . . *Gustave Colline, the great philosopher; Marcel, the great painter; Rudolph, the great poet, and Schaunard, the great musician—as they were wont to style them selves—regularly frequented the Cafe Momus, where, being inseparable, they were nicknamed 'The Four Musketeers.'*

"*Indeed, they always went about together, played together, dined together, often without paying the bill, yet always with a beautiful harmony worthy of the Conservatoire Orchestra.*

"*Mademoiselle Musetta was a pretty girl of twenty.*

"*Very coquettish, rather ambitious, but without any pretensions to spelling.*

"*Oh! those delightful suppers in the Quartier Latin!*

"*A perpetual alternative between a blue brougham and an omnibus; between the Rue Breda and the Quartier Latin.*

". . . *Well! what of that? From time to time I feel the need of breathing the atmosphere of such a life as this. My madcap existence is like a song; each of my love-episodes forms a verse of it, but Marcel is its refrain!*"

Act II

In the Latin Quarter

Christmas Eve

A conflux of streets; where they meet, a square, flanked by shops of all sorts; on one side the Café Momus.

Aloof from the crowd, RUDOLPH *and* MIMI; COLLINE *is near a rag-shop,* SCHAUNARD *stands outside a tinker's, buying a pipe and a horn,* MARCEL *is being hustled hither and thither.*

A vast, motley crowd; soldiers, serving maids, boys, girls, children, students, work girls, gendarmes, etc. It is evening. The shops are decked with tiny lamps; a huge lantern lights up the entrance to the Café Momus. The café is so crowded that some of the customers are obliged to seat themselves outside.

HAWKERS: (*outside their shops*)
    Come, buy my oranges!
    Hot roasted chestnuts!
    Trinkets and crosses!
    Fine hardbake!
    Excellent toffee!
    Flowers for the ladies!
    Try our candy!
    Cream for the babies!
    Fat larks and ortolans!
    Look at them!
    Fine salmon!
    Look at our chestnuts!
    Who'll buy my carrots?
THE CROWD:
CITIZENS: What a racket!
WOMEN: What uproar!
STUDENTS AND WORK GIRLS:
    Hold fast to me; come along!
A MOTHER: (*calling her children*) Lisa! Emma!
CITIZENS: Ho! make way there!

THE MOTHER: Emma, don't you hear me?

STUDENTS AND WORK GIRLS: Rue Mazarin's the nearest.

WOMEN: Let's get away, I'm choking!

CITIZENS: See! the café is near!

(*At the Caf*é)

CITIZENS:

Come here, waiter!

Come along!

Come along!

Come here!

To me!

Some beer!

A glass!

Vanilla!

Come along!

Come along!

Some beer!

Some coffee!

Hurry up!

SCH.: (*blowing the horn*)

D! D! D! what a dreadful D!

(*Haggling with the tinker*)

What's the price of the lot?

COL.: (*to the clothes dealer, who has been mending a jacket for him*)

It's rather shabby, but sound and not expensive.

(*He pays, and then carefully consigns the books to the various pockets of his long coat*)

(MARCEL *alone in the midst of the crowd, with a parcel under his arm, making eyes at the girls who jostle against him in the crowd*)

MAR.: I feel somehow as if I fain must shout:

Ho! laughing lassies, will you play at love?

Let's play together, let's play the game of buy and sell:

Who'll give a penny for my guileless heart?

(*Pushing through the crowd,* RUDOLPH *and* MIMI, *arm in arm, approach a bonnet shop*)

RUD.: Let's go!

MIMI: To buy the bonnet?

RUD.: Hold tightly to my arm, love!

(*They enter the bonnet shop*)

(SCHAUNARD *strolls about in front of the Café Momus, waiting for his friends, and, armed with his huge pipe and hunting horn, he watches the crowd curiously*)

SCH.: Surging onward—eager, breathless—

    Moves the madding crowd,

    As they frolic ever

    In their wild, insane endeavor.

COL.: (*comes up, waving an old book in triumph*)

    Such a rare copy! well-nigh unique,

    A grammar of Runic!

SCH.: (*who arrives at that moment behind* COLLINE, *compassionately*)

    Honest fellow!

MAR.: (*arriving at the Café Momus, and finding* SCHAUNARD *and* COLLINE)

    To supper!

SCH. AND COL.: Ho! Rudolph!

MAR.: He's gone to buy a bonnet.

(MARCEL, SCHAUNARD *and* COLLINE *try to find an empty table outside the café, but there is only one, which is occupied by townsfolk. At these latter the three friends glare furiously, and then enter the café. The crowd disperses among the adjacent streets. The shops are crowded and the square becomes densely thronged with buyers who come and go. In the café there is much animation.* RUDOLPH *and* MIMI *come out of the shop*)

RUD.: (*to* MIMI)

    Come along! my friends are waiting.

MIMI: Do you think this rose-trimmed bonnet suits me?

RUD.: The color suits your dark complexion.

MIMI: (*looking into the window of a bonnet shop*) O what a pretty
    necklace!

RUD.: I have an aunt a millionaire.

    If the good God wills to take her,

    Then shall you have a necklace far more fine.

(*suddenly seeing* MIMI *look round suspiciously*)

    What is it?

MIMI: Are you jealous?

RUD.: The man in love is always jealous, darling.

MIMI: Are you then in love?

RUD.: (*squeezing her arm in his*)

    Yes, so much in love!

    Are you?

MIMI: Yes, deeply.

(*Enter from the café,* COLLINE, SCHAUNARD *and* MARCEL *carrying a table. A waiter follows with chairs. The townsfolks seated near seem vexed at the noise which the three friends are making, for they soon get up and walk away*)

COL.: The vulgar herd I hate, just as I did Horace.

SCH.: And I, when I am eating,
    I can't stand being crowded.

MAR.: (*to the waiter*) Smartly!

SCH.: For many!

MAR.: We want a supper of the choicest!

(MIMI *and* RUDOLPH *joining their friends*)

RUD.: (*accompanied by* MIMI) Two places.

COL.: Let's have supper.

RUD.: So we have come. (*introducing Mimi*)
    This is Mimi,
    The merry flower girl;
    And now she's come to join us.
    Our party is completed—
    For I shall play the poet,
    While she's the muse incarnate.
    Forth from my brain flow songs of passion,
    As, at her touch the pretty buds blow;
    As in the soul awaketh beautiful love!

MAR.: (*ironically*) My word, what high falutin'!

COL.: *Digna est intrari.*

SCH.: *Ingrediat si necessit.*

COL.: I'll grant only an *accessit!*

(RUDOLPH *makes* MIMI *sit down. All being seated, the waiter returns with the menu*)

COL.: (*with an air of great importance*) Some sausage!

PAR.: (*faintly in the distance*) Who'll buy some pretty toys from
    Parpignol?

(*Boys and girls running out from the shops and adjoining streets*)

BOYS AND GIRLS: Parpignol! Parpignol!

(*Enter* PARPIGNOL *from the Rue Dauphin, pushing a barrow festooned with foliage, flowers and paper lanterns*)

PAR.: (*crying*) Who'll buy some pretty toys from Parpignol?

CHILDREN, (*crowding and jumping round the barrow*)
    Parpignol! Parpignol!

With his pretty barrow bright with flowers!
(*admiring the toys*)

I want the horn! and I the horse!

Get away, they are mine!

I want the gun! and I the whip!

No, the drum shall be mine!

(*At the cries of the children, the mothers try, but without success, to lead them away from* PARPIGNOL, *scolding loudly*)

MOTHERS:

Ah! wait a bit, you dirty little rascals.

What can it be that sets you all a-gaping?

Get home to your beds, get home, lazy rascals,

Or you shall all have a tidy beating.

(*The children refuse to go. One of them cries for Parpignol's toys and his mother pulls his ear. The mothers, relenting, buy some. Parpignol moves down the street, followed by the children, pretending to play on their toy instruments*)

PAR.: (*in the distance*) Who'll buy some pretty toys of Parpignol!

(*The waiter presents the menu, which the four friends carefully scrutinize in turn*)

SCH.: Bring some venison.

MAR.: I'll have turkey.

RUD.: (*in an undertone to* MIMI) Mimi, what would you like?

MIMI: Some custard!

SCH.: And some Rhenish!

COL.: Bring some claret, too!

SCH.: And some lobster, only shell it!

The best you've got—for a lady!

MAR.: (*disconcerted at the sight of* MUSETTA; *to the waiter*)

And I'll have a phial of poison! (*throwing himself on a chair*)

SCH., COL. AND RUD.: (*turning on hearing* MARCEL'S *exclamation*)

Oh! Musetta!

(*the friends look pityingly at* MARCEL, *who turns pale*)

(*The shopwomen are going away, but stop to watch the fair stranger, and are astonished to recognize in her* MUSETTA; *they whisper among themselves, pointing at her*)

Look! 'tis Musetta!

She!

Musetta!

'Tis she!

Yes!

Yes!

'Tis Musetta!

Oh! what swagger!

My! she's gorgeous.

(*entering their shops*)

STUDENTS AND WORK GIRLS (*crossing the stage*)

Only look! why, there she is!

Some old stammering dotard's with her, too!

Yes, 'tis she!

'Tis she!

Musetta!

(*Enter from the corner of the Rue Mazarin an extremely pretty coquettish-looking young lady. She is followed by a pompous old gentleman, who is both fussy and over-dressed*)

ALCINDORO DE MITONNEAUX: (*joining* MUSETTA, *out of breath*)

Just like a valet

I must run here and there.

No, no, not for me!

I can stand it no more.

(MUSETTA *without noticing* ALCINDORO, *takes a vacant seat, outside the café*) How now? Outside? Here?

MUS.: (*without noticing his protests, he fearing to remain outside in the cold*) Sit down, Lulu!

ALC.: (*in great irritation, sits down, and turns up his coat collar*)

Such a term of fond endearment

Pray do not apply to me!

MUS.: Now, don't be Blue Beard, pray!

(*A waiter approaches briskly, to prepare the table and begins to serve.* SCHAUNARD *and* COLLINE *furtively watch* MUSETTA. MARCEL *feigns the greatest indifference.* RUDOLPH *devotes all his attention to* MIMI)

SCH.: (*at the sight of the old gentleman with his decorations*)

He's had a pretty good dose, I reckon.

COL.: (*scrutinizing* ALCINDORO) The naughty, naughty elder!

MAR.: (*contemptuously*) With his good young Susanna.

MIMI: (*to* RUDOLPH) And her clothes are smart, too!

RUD.: The angels can't afford them.

(*A piquet of the National Guard passes across the square; some shop-keepers go home; at the corner of the street the chestnut-seller does a thriving trade;*

the old clothes dealer fills her barrel with clothes, and goes away with it over her shoulder)

Mus.: (*disconcerted at not being noticed by her friends*)

 Marcel can see me,

 But he won't look, the villain!

 And Schaunard!

 They provoke me past bearing!

 Ah! could I but beat them!

 If I could, I would scratch!

 But I only have to back me

 This old pelican!

 No matter! (*calls the waiter who has gone away*)

 Hi! waiter, here! (*the waiter hurriedly approaches*)

 See, this plate has a horrid smell of onions!

(*dashes the plate on the ground; the waiter picks up the pieces*)

Alc.: Don't, Musetta! do be quiet!

Mus.: (*irritated, still watching* Marcel) He won't look round! Now I could beat him!

Alc.: What's the matter?

Mus.: (*sharply*) I meant the waiter!

Alc.: Manners! Manners!

(*Takes the bill from the waiter and orders the supper*)

Mus.: (*more irritated*)

 Such a bore!

 Just let me have my own way.

 If you please; I won't be ruled by you!

Mimi: (*looking curiously at* Rudolph) Do you know who she is?

Mar.: You had better ask me.

 Well, her name is Musetta

 Her surname is Temptation.

 As to her vocation:

 Like a rose in the breezes,

 So she changes lover for lover without number.

 And like the spiteful screech owl,

 A bird that's most rapacious,

 The food that most she favors is the heart!

 Her food the heart is;

 Thus have I now none left!

(*to his friends, concealing his agitation*)

So pass me the ragout!

SCH.: (*to* COLLINE)

Now the fun's at its climax,

To one she speaks because the other listens.

COL.: (*to* SCHAUNARD)

The other will not hear,

Feigns not to see the girl: which makes her mad.

RUD.: (*to* MIMI)

Now let me tell you

I never would forgive you.

MIMI: (*to* RUDOLPH)

I love you, love you fondly,

Am wholly yours, my dearest! (*eating*)

COL.: What's that about forgiveness?

(*coquettishly watching* MARCEL, *who becomes agitated*)

MUS.: (*watching* MARCEL; *in a loud voice to* MARCEL) Why, don't you
know me?

ALC.: (*thinking* MUSETTA *spoke to him*) Well, I'm giving the order,
dear.

MUS.: (*as above*) But your heart is a-throbbing!

ALC.: (*as above*) Not so loud.

MUS.: (*to herself*) But your heart is a-throbbing!

ALC.: Do be quiet!

MUS.: As through the streets I wander onward merrily,

See how the folk look round,

Because they know I'm charming,

A very charming girl.

And then 'tis mine to mark the hidden longing,

And all the passion in their eyes;

And then the joy of conquest overcomes me,

Every man is my prize!

And thus their hearts, their hearts I capture,

As if by magic all my own, ah! rapture!

Tis mine alone!

Now you that once your love for me betrayed,

Why should you be dismayed?

Yet though deep in your heart

Rankles the smart.

You'd ne'er confess—but rather die!

GIUSEPPE GIACOSA AND LUIGI ILLICA

(SCHAUNARD *and* COLLINE *rise and stand aside, watching the scene with interest, while* RUDOLPH *and* MIMI *remain seated and continue their talk.* MARCEL *nervously quits his seat, and is about to go, but is spell-bound by* MUSETTA'S *voice*)

ALC.: This odious singing upsets me entirely!

(ALCINDORO *vainly endeavors to induce* MUSETTA *to resume her seat at the table where the supper is ready*)

MIMI: (*to* RUDOLPH)

> Oh! now I see that this unhappy maiden
> Adores your friend Marcel madly!

RUD.: She once was Marcel's love;

> She wantonly forsook her fate,
> And rarer game she thought to capture!

MIMI: The love that's born of passion ends in grief;

> That poor, unhappy girl!
> She moves me to tears!

RUD.: Who can revive a love that's dead?

MAR.: Hold me back! hold me back!

COL.: Who knows what will happen now?

> Goodness me! 'tis most unpleasant!
> Anyhow, it is for me!
> She is pretty, I don't doubt it;
> Yet I would rather have
> My pipe and a page of Homer!

SCH.: See the braggart in a moment will give in;

> The snare for some is pleasant,
> For the biter and the bit.

(*to* COLLINE)

> If such a pretty damsel
> Should but make eyes at you,
> You'd forget your mouldy classics,
> And run to fetch her shoe.

MUS.: Ah! Marcel you are vanquished!

> And though your heart is breaking,
> You'd never let us know, (*feigning great regret*)

(*I must try to get rid of the old boy*)

> Oh! dear!

ALC.: What now?

MUS.: How it pains me! how it pains me!

ALC.: Let's see!

MUS.: My foot!

 Break it, tear it,

 I can't bear it,

 Do, I implore you!

ALC.: (*bending down to untie her shoe*) Gently, gently!

MUS.: Close by there is a boot-shop; hasten! quickly!

 He may have boots to please me.

ALC.: What imprudence!

MUS.: Ah! the torture!

 How these horrid tight shoes squeeze me!

 I'll take it off! So let it lie!

ALC.: What will people say?

 What imprudence!

SCH. AND COL:

 Now the fun becomes stupendous

 In truth, 'tis better than a play!

MUS.: Hasten, hasten! Bring another pair! Go!

ALC.: What imprudence!

 Nothing short of scandal!

 Musetta, shame!

(*Hides her shoe under his coat, which he hastily buttons up; hurries off the stage*)

MAR.: (*greatly agitated*)

 Ah! golden youth! you are not dead, not dead for me,

 For love revives again in me;

 If at my door you came to greet me,

 My heart would straight go out to meet thee!

(MUSETTA *and* MARCEL *embrace with much fervor*)

MUS.: Marcel!

MAR.: Enchantress!

SCH.: This is the final tableau! (*A waiter brings in the bill*)

RUD., COL. AND SCH.: The bill!

SCH.: What a bother!

COL.: Who bade him bring it?

SCH.: Let's see.

(*Drums heard in the distance*)

RUD. AND COL.: Out with your coppers!

SCH.: Out with your coppers,

 Colline, Rudolph, and you, Marcel.

MAR.: We've not a rap!

SCH.: I say!

RUD.: I've thirty sous, no more.

MAR., SCH. AND COL.: I say! no more than that?

STREET ARABS, (*hastening from the right*) 'Tis the Tattoo!

WORK GIRLS, (*hastening out of the café*) 'Tis the Tattoo!

STUDENTS AND CITIZENS: 'Tis the Tattoo!

(*Hastening from the left. As the Tattoo is still a long way off, the folk run hither and thither, as if uncertain from which quarter the band will appear*)

SCH.: But who has got my purse?

(*They all feel their pockets which are empty; none can explain the sudden disappearance of* SCHAUNARD's *purse, and they look at each other in surprise*)

STREET ARABS: Will they come along this way?

WORK GIRLS AND STUDENTS: No; from there.

STREET ARABS: They are coming down this way.

WORK GIRLS AND STUDENTS: Here they come!

CITIZENS: Way there!

HAWKERS: Way there!

SOME BOYS: Oh! let me see!

OTHERS: Oh! let me hear!

BOYS: Mother, do let me see!

OTHERS: Papa, do let me hear!

MOTHERS: Lisette, do be quiet!

    Tony, do have done! do be quiet!

MUS.: (*to the waiter*)

    And my bill, please, bring to me.

(*To waiter who brings the bill*)

    Thank you.

    Just make one bill of the two.

    The gentleman will pay

    Who came to sup with me.

RUD., MAR., SCH. AND COL.: Yes, he will pay!

MAR.: (*aside*) He will pay!

SCH. AND COL.: Yes, he will pay!

MUS.: (*placing both bills at* ALCINDORO's *place*)

    And, after this pleasant meeting,

    This shall be my greeting!

RUD., MAR., SCH. AND COL.: And, after our pleasant meeting,

    This shall be her greeting!

(*The crowd fills the stage and the patrol advances gradually*)

WORK GIRLS: They will come along this way.

STUDENTS, CITIZENS AND HAWKERS: Yes, this way!

STREET ARABS: When it gets nearer,
   We'll march along beside it.

(*Several windows are opened at which mothers and their children appear and eagerly await the coming of the patrol*)

HAWKERS: In that patrol perceive
   The country's noble might!

STREET ARABS: Now, look out! they're coming!

STUDENTS, WORK GIRLS AND CITIZENS: Do stand back, for here they come!

MAR.: See, the patrol is coming!

COL.: Look out that old boy
   Don't catch you with his darling!

RUD.: See, the patrol is coming!

MAR. AND SCH.: Now the crowd is tremendous:
   T' escape will be so easy.

(*The patrol enters, headed by a gigantic drum-major, who dexterously twists his baton, showing the way*)

STREET ARABS AND WORK GIRLS: And there's the drum-major!

CITIZENS AND SHOP-KEEPERS: As proud as a warrior of old!

MIMI, MUS. AND RUD.: Quick, or you will miss them!

MAR., SCH. AND COL.: Quick, or you will miss them!

STREET ARABS AND HAWKERS: The drum-major, look! what a dandy!

STUDENTS AND WORK GIRLS: What swagger! What a figure!

STREET ARABS: There go the sappers!

CITIZENS: What a dandy!

STUDENTS AND CITIZENS: Like a general he appears!
   He passes by and heeds us not!

WORK GIRLS: Like a general he appears!
   Of all our hearts the conqueror!

(MUSETTA *being without her shoe, cannot walk, so* MARCEL *and* COLLINE *carry her through the crowd, as they endeavor to follow the patrol. The mob, seeing her borne along in this triumphal fashion, give her a regular ovation.* MARCEL *and* COLLINE *with* MUSETTA *follow the patrol;* RUDOLPH *and* MIMI *follow arm in arm;* SCHAUNARD *goes next, blowing his horn; while the students, work-girls, street-lads, women and towns-folk merrily bring up the rear*)

(Marching in time with the music, the whole vast crowd gradually moves off as it follows the patrol. Meanwhile ALCINDORO, *with a pair of shoes carefully wrapped up, returns to the café in search of* MUSETTA. *The waiter by the table takes up the bill left by* MUSETTA *and ceremoniously hands it to* ALCINDORO, *who, seeing the amount, and perceiving that they have all left him there alone, falls back into a chair, utterly dumbfounded)*

"Mimi's voice seemed to go through Rudolph's heart like a death-knell. His love for her was a jealous, fantastic, weird, hysterical love. Scores of times they were on the point of separating.

"It must be admitted that their existence was a veritable 'hell-up-on-earth.'

"Thus (if life it was) did they live; a few happy days alternating with many wretched ones, while perpetually awaiting a divorce."

"Either as a congenital defect or as a natural instinct, Musetta possessed a positive genius for elegance.

"Even in her cradle this strange creature must surely have asked for a mirror.

"Intelligent, shrewd, and above all, hostile to anything that she considered tyranny, she had but one rule—caprice.

"In truth the only man that she really loved was Marcel; perhaps because he alone could make her suffer. Yet extravagance was for her one of the conditions of well-being."

Act III

Beyond the toll-gate, the outer boulevard is formed in the background by the Orleans high-road, half hidden by tall houses and the misty gloom of February. To the left is a tavern with a small open space in front of the toll-gate. To the right is the Boulevard d'Enfer; to the left, that of St. Jacques.

On the right also there is the entrance of the Rue d'Enfer, leading to the Quartier Latin.

Over the tavern, as its sign-board, hangs MARCEL's *picture, "The Passage of the Red Sea," while underneath, in large letters, is the inscription. "At the Port of Marseilles." On either side of the door are frescoes of a Turk and a Zouave with a huge laurel-wreath round his fez. From the ground-floor windows of the tavern, which faces the toll-gate, light gleams. The plane-trees, grey and gaunt, which flank the toll-gate square, lead diagonally towards the two boulevards. Between each tree is a marble bench. It is towards the close of February; snow covers all.*

As the curtain rises, the scene is merged in the dim light of early dawn. In front of a brazier are seated, in a group, snoring custom-house officers. From the tavern at intervals one may hear laughter, shouts, and the clink of glasses. A custom-house official comes out of the tavern with wine. The toll-gate is closed.

Behind the toll-gate, stamping their feet and blowing in their frost-bitten fingers, stand several street-scavengers.

SCAVENGERS: What ho, there! What ho, there! Admit us!
    Make haste and let us pass,
    The sweepers are we. (*stamping their feet*)
    Look how it's snowing! What ho, there!
    We are frozen!
AN OFFICIAL: (*yawning and stretching himself*) All right!
(*Goes to open the gate; the scavengers pass through to the Rue d'Enfer. The official closes the gate again*)
CHORUS: (*from the tavern; the clink of glasses forms an accompaniment to the song*)
    Pass the glass,
    Let each toast his lass;
    Pass the glass,
    Let each lad toast his lass;

Ha! Ha!
Each one as he sips,
As he sips his wine,
Shall dream of lips
Made for love divine!

Mus.: (*from the tavern*)
Ah!
As the toper loves his glass,
So the gallant loves his lass.

Chorus: (*all bursting into laughter*) Noah and Eve!

Milk Women: (*from within*) Houp-la! Houp-la!

(*A sergeant comes out of the guard-house and orders the toll-gate to be opened*)

Custom House Official: Here come the women with their milk.

(*A tinkling of cart-bells is heard*)

Carters: (*from within*) Houp-la!

(*Carts pass along the outer boulevard, lighted by large lanterns*)

Milk Women: (*quite close*) Houp-la!

(*The gloom gradually gives way to daylight*)

Milk Women: (*to the officials who admit them to the toll-gate*)
Good-morrow!

Peasant Women: (*who enter carrying baskets*)
Butter! Cheese!
Chickens and eggs!

Some: Which way, then, are you going?

Others: Up to Saint Michael's.

Some: Well, shall we see you later?

Others: At twelve o'clock.

(*They go off in various directions, and the officials remove the bench and brazier*)

(*Enter Mimi from the Rue d'Enfer; she looks about her as if anxious to make sure of her whereabouts. On reaching the first plane-tree she is seized by a violent fit of coughing. Then recovering herself, she sees the sergeant, whom she approaches*)

Mimi: Oh! Please, sir, tell me the name of that tavern
Where now a painter's working?

Sergeant: (*pointing to the tavern*) There it is.

Mimi: Thank you.

(*A serving woman comes out of the tavern; Mimi goes to her*)
Oh! my good woman, pray do me this favor!

Can you find me the painter, Marcel?
I fain would see him; the matter's urgent;
Just tell him softly that Mimi awaits him.

SERGEANT: (*to a passer-by*) Ho! there! What's in the basket?

OFFICIAL: (*after searching the basket*) Empty.

SERGEANT: Pass, there!

(*Other folk now pass through the toll-gate and move off in different directions. The bell of the Hospice Ste. Therese rings for matins*)

MAR.: (*coming out of the inn*) Mimi!

MIMI: I hoped that I should find you here.

MAR.: Aye, here we've been for a month:
So to pay for our footing,
Musetta teaches singing
To those who come here.
And I, well—I paint warriors—
There, on the house front!

MIMI: Where is Rudolph?

MAR.: Here. 'Tis bitter, pray enter!

MIMI: (*bursting into tears*)
Enter I cannot, no!

MAR.: Why not?

MIMI: Oh! good Marcel! oh! help me!

MAR.: Say, what has happened?

MIMI: Rudolph is madly jealous!
He loves and yet avoids me!
A glance, a touch, a token,
Suffice to make him jealous,
And start his senseless fury!
And oft at night,
When feigning to be sleeping,
I felt his eyes were watching
to spy upon my slumbers!
How oft he would reproach me!
"You are not mine, Mimi!
You love another gallant!"
Alas! 'tis jealousy that prompts him.
Yet how may I reply?

MAR.: Two that live thus, I reckon,
Would be surely better parted.

Mimi: You are right, you speak truly:
'Twere best we were parted.
Will you aid us, then,
Will you aid us to part?
Oft to do this we have striven, but in vain.
Ah! 'tis true, to part were the best.

Mar.: I'm happy with Musetta,
And she's happy with me.
Because 'tis mirth that binds us together.
Laughter, music and song,
Ever our love prolong.

Mimi: Ah! then, aid us, I pray you!

Mar.: 'Tis well, 'tis well! Now will I wake him.

Mimi: Wake him?

Mar.: Overcome with fatigue,
Just as dawn was approaching,
On the bench fast lie slumbers,
(*Motions* Mimi *to look through the tavern window*)
Behold him! (Mimi *coughs persistently*)
What coughing!

Mimi: Unceasingly it shakes me,
And Rudolph now forsakes me.
And says to me, "It is over!"
At daybreak swift escaping,
I hurried here to find him.

Mar.: (*watching* Rudolph *inside the tavern*)
He's moving, waking, and wants me.
Come, then.

Mimi: He must not see me.

Mar.: Well, hide yourself out there.
(*Points to the plane-trees.* Mimi *hides behind the trees*)

Rud.: (*coming out of the inn, hastens towards* Marcel)
Marcel! at last I've found you,
Where none can hear us.
I want a separation from Mimi.

Mar.: Is that your latest whim?

Rud.: Love in my heart was dying, almost was dead,
But her blue eyes new glory on me shed.
Love, swift revived, all me; what woe is mine!

GIUSEPPE GIACOSA AND LUIGI ILLICA

MAR.: Ah! would you now such bitter pain recall?
(MIMI *warily approaches to listen*)
RUD.: Yes, always.
MAR.: Nay, be prudent! Love is not worth the keeping,
    That only ends in weeping.
    Love must thrive in mirth and gladness,
    Or else it is but madness.
    'Tis that you're jealous!
RUD.: Aye, somewhat;
    And choleric, and lunatic,
    And a victim of vile suspicion,
    Unhappy, and stubborn!
MIMI: (*aside*)
    He's getting in a rage;
    Poor little Mimi!
RUD.: Mimi's a heartless maiden,
    Prone to flirting with all.
    A scented dandy, some lordling,
    Now striveth to win her caresses.
    With bosom swaying,
    One foot displaying,
    Doth she lure him on
    With the magic of her smile.
MAR.: Shall I be frank? I think 'tis hardly true.
RUD.: No, 'tis not true.
    In vain, in vain I smother
    All the torture that racks me.
    I love Mimi, she is my only treasure!
    I love her, but, oh! I fear it!
(*Mimi surprised, comes closer and closer, under cover of the trees*)
    Mimi's so sickly, so ailing,
    Every day she grows weaker,
    The poor girl, as I think, is dying.
MAR.: (*fearing* MIMI *may overhear them, tries to keep* RUDOLPH *further off*) Oh! Rudolph!
MIMI: What's he saying?
RUD.: By fierce, incessant coughing
    Her fragile frame is shaken,
    While in her cheeks so pallid

The fires of fever waken.

MAR.: (*agitated, perceiving that* MIMI *is listening*) Softly!

MIMI: (*weeping*) Woe is me! I'm dying!

RUD.: And my room's but a squalid hovel,
    No fire there burneth,
    Only the cruel night wind
    Waileth, waileth there ever.
    Yet she's merry and smiling,
    While, remorseful, despairing,
    I feel that 'tis I that am guilty.

MAR.: (*eager to draw* RUDOLPH *aside*) List but a moment!

MIMI: (*disconsolately*) Ah! I'm dying!

RUD.: Mimi's a hot-house flower!

MAR.: Nay, but listen!

MIMI: Ah me! ah me!
    All is over, life and loving,
    All are ended!
    Mimi must die!

MAR.: Softly!

RUD.: Want has wasted her beauty,
    And to bring her back to life
    Would need far more than love.

MAR.: Nay, Rudolph, but listen!

(*Mimi's violent coughing and sobbing reveal her presence*)

RUD.: Ha! Mimi! You here!
    You heard, you heard me?
    Swayed by each light suspicion,
    A trifle yet alarms me;
    Come, come inside here!

(*Seeks to take her into the tavern*)

MIMI: No, that odor is stifling me!

RUD.: (*affectionately embracing her*) Ah, Mimi!

(*From the tavern Musetta's brazen laugh is heard*)

MAR.: (*running to look through the window*)
    Tis Musetta that's laughing!
    Laughing, flirting!
    Ah! what a hussy!
    I'll not allow it. (*enters the tavern impetuously*)

MIMI: (*disengaging herself from* RUDOLPH's *embrace*) Farewell!

Rud.: (*surprised*) What! Going?

Mimi: To the home that she left
    At the voice of her lover.
    Sad, forsaken Mimi
    Must turn back, heavy-hearted.
    For love and her lover
    Are gone, and she must die,
    Farewell, then!
    I wish you well!
    Nay, listen! listen! those things,
    Those few old things I've left behind me,
    Within my trunk safely arc stored.
    That bracelet of gold,
    The prayer-book you gave me,
    Pray wrap them up together in my little apron,
    And I will send to fetch them.
    Yet stay! Beneath the pillow
    You'll find my little bonnet—
    Who knows?
    Maybe you'd like to keep it
    To remind you of our love!
    Farewell! Good-bye! I wish you well!

Rud.: Then, you are going to leave me?
    Yes, you are going, my little Mimi?
    Ah! farewell, sweet dream of love!

Mimi: Farewell! farewell!
    Glad awakenings in the morning!

Rud.: Farewell, our sweet love that vanished,
    Yet that your smile reviveth!

Mimi: (*playfully*) Farewell to jealousy and fury!
    Farewell suspicion, and its bitter anguish!

Rud.: Kisses sweet that, as poet,
    I bought back with caresses!

Mimi and Rud.: Lonely in winter,
    With Death as sole companion!
    But in glad springtime
    There's the sun, the glorious sun!

(*From the tavern the sound of breaking plates and glasses is heard*)

Mus.: (*from within*) What d'ye mean? What d'ye mean? (*running out*)

Mar.: (*from within*)

    You were laughing, you were flirting

    By the fireside with that stranger!

(*stopping on the threshold of the inn and confronting* Musetta)

    And how you colored

    When I caught you in the corner!

Mus.: (*defiantly*) Stuff and nonsense! all he said was:

    "Are you very fond of dancing?"

    And, half blushing, I made answer:

    "I'd be dancing all day long, sir."

Mar.: This is talk that only leads to things dishonest.

Mus.: My own way I mean to have!

Mar.: (*half menacing* Musetta)

    I will teach you better manners;

    Now if I catch you once more flirting—

Mus.: What a bother!

    Why this anger?

    Why this fury?

    We're not married yet, thank goodness!

Mar.: You shall not do as you like, miss!

    I will stop your little game!

Mus.: I abhor that sort of lover

    Who pretends he is your husband!

Mar.: I'm not going to be your blockhead,

    Just because you're fond of flirting!

Mus.: I shall flirt just when it suits me!

Mar.: You're most frivolous, Musetta!

Mus.: Yes, I shall! yes, I shall!

    I shall flirt just when it suits me!

Mar.: You can go, and God be with you!

Mus.: Musetta's going away;

    Yes, going away!

Mar.: And for me 'tis a good riddance!

Mus.: Fare you well, sir!

Mar.: Fare you well, ma'am!

Mus.: I say farewell with all my heart!

Mar.: Farewell, ma'am, pray begone!

(*She retreats in a fury, but suddenly stops*)

Mus.: (*shouting*) Go back and paint your house front!

MAR.: Viper! (*enters the tavern*)

MUS.: Toad! (*exit*)

MIMI: I'm so happy in the spring!

RUD.: As comrades you've lilies and roses.

MIMI: Forth from each nest
    Comes a murmur of birdlets!

RUD. AND MIMI: When the hawthorn-bough's in blossom,
    When we have the glorious sun,
    Murmur the silver fountains,
    The breezes of the evening
    Waft fragrant balsams
    To the world and its sorrow.
    Shall we await another spring?

MIMI: (*moving away with* RUDOLPH) Always yours forever!

RUD. *and* MIMI: Our time for parting's when the roses blow!

MIMI: Ah! that our winter might last forever!

RUD. *and* MIMI: Our time for parting's when the roses blow!

"At that period, indeed, for some time past, the friends had led lonely lives.

"Musetta had once more become a sort of semi-official personage; for three or four months Marcel had never met her.

"And Mimi, too, no word of her had Rudolph ever heard except when he talked about her to himself when he was alone.

"One day, as Marcel furtively kissed a bunch of ribbons that Musetta had left behind, he saw Rudolph hiding away a bonnet, that same pink bonnet which Mimi had forgotten.

"'Good!' muttered Marcel, 'he's as craven-hearted as I am.'"

* * * * *

"A gay life, yet a terrible one."

Act IV

In the Attic

(*As in Act I*)
(MARCEL, *as before, stands in front of his easel, while* RUDOLPH *sits at his writing table; each trying to make the other believe that he is working indefatigably, whereas they are really only gossiping*)

MAR.: (*resuming his talk*) In a coupé?
RUD.: Yes, in carriage and pair did she merrily hail me.
    "Well, Musetta," I questioned:
    "How's your heart?"
    "It beats not—or I don't feel it—Thanks
      to this velvet I'm wearing!"
MAR.: (*endeavoring to laugh*) I'm glad, very glad!
RUD.: (*aside*) You humbug, you! You're fretting and fuming!
MAR.: It beats not! Bravo!
(*commences to paint with great vigor*)
    Then I saw, too—
RUD.: Musetta?
MAR.: Mimi.
RUD.: You saw her? How strange! (*stops painting*)
MAR.: Rode in her carriage in grand apparel.
    Just like a duchess.
RUD.: Delightful! I'm glad to hear it.
MAR.: (*aside*) You liar! you're pining with love.
RUD. AND MAR.: Now to work! (*they go on working*)
RUD.: (*throwing down his pen*) This pen's too awful!
(*remains seated, apparently lost in thought*)
MAR.: (*flinging away his brush*) This infamous paint-brush!
(*Stares at his canvas, and then without* RUDOLPH *observing it, he takes from his pocket a bunch of ribbons and kisses it*)
RUD.: Ah! Mimi! false, fickle-hearted!
    Ah! beauteous days departed!
    Those hands so dainty!
    Oh! fragrant, shining tresses!

Ah! snow-white bosom!

Ah! Mimi! those brief, glad, golden days!

MAR.: (*putting away his ribbons and staring anew at his canvas*)

How is it that my brush

With speed mechanical keeps moving,

And plasters on the colors

Quite against my will?

And though I would be painting landscapes,

Meadows, woodlands fair in Spring-tide,

My brush refuses to perform its office;

But paints dark eyes, and two red, smiling lips;

The features of Musetta haunt me still!

RUD.: (*taking Mimi's old bonnet from the table drawer*)

And thou, O! rose-pink bonnet,

That 'neath her pillow lay,

That in her hour of parting she forgot—Thou

wert the witness of our joy!

Come to my heart, ah! come!

Lie close against my heart, since my love is dead!

(*clasps the bonnet to his heart*)

MAR.: Ah! frivolous Musetta! thee can I ne'er forget!

My grief affords her pleasure,

And yet my weak heart is fain

To call her to my fond arms again.

RUD.: (*endeavoring to conceal his emotion from Marcel, carelessly questions him*) What time is it now?

MAR.: (*roused from his reverie, gaily replies*) Time for our yesterday's dinner.

RUD.: But Schaunard's not back yet. (*Enter Schaunard and Colline; the former carries four rolls, and the latter a paper bag*)

SCH.: Here we are!

RUD.: How now?

MAR.: How now?

(SCHAUNARD *places the rolls on the table*)

MAR.: (*disdainfully*) Some bread!

COL.: (*taking a herring out of the bag, and putting it on the table*)

A dish that's worthy of Demosthenes:

'Tis a herring!

SCH.: 'Tis salted!

Col.: 'Our dinner is ready!

(*Seating themselves at the table, they pretend to be having a sumptuous meal*)

Mar.: This is a food that the gods might envy.

Sch.: (*placing Colline's hat on the table, and thrusting a bottle of water into it*) Now the champagne in the ice must go.

Rud.: (*to* Marcel, *offering him some bread*)

    Choose, my lord marquis—salmon or turbot?

(*His offer is accepted, when, turning to* Schaunard, *he proffers another crust of bread*)

    Now, duke, here's a choice vol-au-vent with mushrooms. (*He politely declines, and pours out a glass of water, which he hands to Marcel*)

Sch.: Thank you, I dare not, this evening I'm dancing! (*The one and only tumbler is handed about. Colline, after voraciously devouring his roll, rises*)

Rud.: (*to Colline*) What? sated?

Col.: (*with an air of great importance*) To business! The king awaits me.

Mar.: (*eagerly*) What plot is brewing?

Rud.: What's in the wind?

Sch.: (*rises and approaches Colline, observing with droll inquisitiveness*) What's in the wind?

Mar.: What's in the wind?

(Colline *struts up and down, full of self-importance*)

Col.: The king requires my services.

(*The others surround* Colline, *bowing low to him*)

Sch.: Bravo!

Mar.: Bravo!

Rud.: Bravo!

Col.: (*with a patronizing air*) And then I've got to see Guizot!

Sch.: Give me a goblet.

Mar.: (*giving him the only glass*) Aye, quaff now a bumper!

Sch.: (*solemnly gets on to a chair and raises his glass*) Have I permission, oh! my most noble courtier?

Rud. and Col.: (*interrupting*) Stop that.

Col.: No more fooling.

Mar.: Stop that. No more nonsense.

Col.: Give me that tumbler. (*taking the glass from* Schaunard)

Sch.: (*motioning his friends to let him speak*) With ardor irresistible Poetry fills my spirit.

COL. AND MAR.: (*yelling*) No.

SCH.: (*complacently*) Then something choreographic may suit you!

RUD., MAR. AND COL.: Yes, yes!

(*Amid applause they surround Schaunard and make him get off the chair*)

SCH.: Some dancing, accompanied by singing?

COL.: Well, clear the stage for action.

(*Moving chairs and tables aside, they prepare for a dance; they suggest various dances*)

COL.: Gavotte.

MAR.: Minuet.

RUD.: Pavanella.

SCH.: (*imitating a Spanish measure*) Fandango.

COL.: I vote we dance quadrilles first. (*the others approve*)

RUD.: Now take your partners.

COL.: I'll lead it. (*pretends to be very busy arranging a quadrille*)

SCH.: (*improvising, beats time with comic pomposity of manner*)
    La-lera, la-lera, la-lera!

RUD.: (*approaching* MARCEL, *and bowing very low, offers him his hand as he gallantly says*) Oh! maiden fair and gentle!

MAR.: (*with coy bashfulness of manner, counterfeiting a woman's voice*)
    My modesty respect, sir, I beg you.

SCH.: Lal-lera, lal-lera, lal-lera, la!

COL.: (*giving directions as to the figures, while* RUDOLPH *and* MARCEL *dance the quadrille*) Balancez!

MAR.: (*in his ordinary voice*) Lal-lera, lal-lera, lal-lera!

SCH.: (*teasingly*) First there's the Rond.

COL.: No, stupid!

SCH.: (*with exaggerated contempt*) You've manners like a clown!

COL.: (*offended*) As I take it, you're insulting!
    Draw your sword, sir!

(*rushes to the fireplace and seizes the tongs*)

SCH.: (*taking up the poker*) Ready! Have at you! (*preparing to receive his adversary's attack*)
    Thy hot blood would I drink!

COL.: (*doing likewise*) One of us shall now be gutted! (RUDOLPH *and* MARCEL *stop dancing and burst out laughing*)

SCH.: Now get a stretcher ready.

COL.: And get a grave-yard, too.

(SCHAUNARD *and* COLLINE *fight*)

Rud. and Mar.: (*gaily*) While they beat each other's brains out, Our
  fandango we will finish.

(*They dance round the combatants, whose blows fall faster. The door opens
and Musetta enters in a state of great agitation*)

Mar.: (*amazed*) Musetta! (*All anxiously cluster round Musetta*)

Mus.: (*hoarsely*) 'Tis Mimi—'tis Mimi who is with me—And is ailing!

Rud.: Mimi!

Mus.: She has not strength to climb the staircase.

(*Through the open door* Rudolph *spies* Mimi, *seated on the topmost stair;
he rushes to her, followed by* Marcel)

Sch.: (*to* Colline) Here's the bed: we'll put her on it.

(*they drag the bed forward*)

Rud.: (*supporting* Mimi *and leading her towards the bed, aided by*
  Marcel) There! some water!

(Musetta *brings a glass of water and makes* Mimi *sip it*)

Mimi: (*passionately*) Oh, Rudolph!

Rud.: Gently, lie down there. (*gently lowers her on the bed*)

Mimi: (*embracing* Rudolph) My darling Rudolph! Ah! let me stay
  with you!

Rud.: Darling Mimi! stay here ever!

(*He induces Mimi to lie down at full length on the bed, and draws the
coverlet over her; he then carefully adjusts the pillow be neath her head*)

Mus.: (*taking the others aside and whispering to them*) I heard them
  saying that Mimi
  Had left the rich old viscount;
  And now was almost dying.
  Ah! but where? After searching,
  I met her alone just now,
  Almost dead with exhaustion.
  She murmured: "I'm dying! dying!
  But listen; I want to die near him.
  Maybe he's waiting!
  Take me thither, Musetta!"

Mar.: Hush! (Musetta *moves farther away from* Mimi)

Mimi: I feel so much better.
  All here seems just the same as ever.

(*with a sweet smile*)

  Ah! It is all so pleasant here!
  Saved from sadness,

All is gladness;

Once again new life is mine!

RUD.: Lips delightful, speak again to me!

Once more enchant me!

MIMI: Ah! beloved! Ah! leave me not!

MUS.: (*aside to the others*) What is there to give her?

MAR.: *and* COL.: Nothing!

MUS.: No coffee? no wine?

MAR.: (*in great dejection*) Nothing; the larder's empty.

SCH.: (*looking closely at Mimi*) In an hour she'll be dead!

MIMI: I feel so cold!

If I had but my muff here!

My poor hands are simply frozen!

How shall I get them warm?

(*Mimi coughs; Rudolph takes her hands in his and chafes them*)

RUD.: In mine, in mine, love!

Silence! for speaking tires you.

MIMI: 'Tis coughing tires me.

I'm used to that, though.

(*seeing* RUDOLPH's *friends, she calls them by name, when they hasten to her side*)

Good-morrow, Marcel!

Schaunard, Colline, good-morrow!

All are here, as I see, glad to welcome Mimi.

RUD.: Hush! Mimi, do not talk.

MIMI: I'll speak low; don't be frightened.

(SCHAUNARD *and* COLLINE *mournfully withdraw; the former sits at the table, burying his face in his hands, the latter is a prey to sad thoughts*)

MIMI: (*motioning Marcel to approach*) Marcel, now believe me,

A good girl is Musetta.

MAR.: (*giving Musetta his hand*) I know, I know.

MUS.: (*drawing Marcel away from Mimi, takes off her earrings and gives them to him as she whispers*) Look here! sell them,

And buy some tonic for her—

Send for a doctor! (MIMI *gradually grows drowsy; Rudolph takes a chair and sits down beside the bed*)

RUD.: Keep quiet.

MIMI: You will not leave me?

RUD.: No, no! (MARCEL *is about to go, when Musetta stops him and takes him still further from Mimi*)

Mus.: Stay, listen! Maybe, what she has asked us
   Will be her last request on earth, little darling!
   I'll go for the muff—I'll come with you.
Mar.: How good you are, Musetta!
(Musetta *and* Marcel *hastily go out*)
Col.: (*who has removed his overcoat while Marcel and Musetta were talking*)
   Garment antique and rusty!
   A last good-bye! farewell!
   Faded friend, so tried and trusty,
   We must part, you and I.
   For never yet your back did you bow
   To rich man or mighty!
   How oft,
   Safe in your pockets spacious,
   Have you concealed philosophers and poets!
   Now that our pleasant friendship is o'er,
   I would bid thee once more,
   Oh! companion tried and trusty,
   Farewell! farewell!
(*He folds up the coat, puts it under his arm, and is about to go, but seeing Schaunard, he approaches him, pats him on the back, and mournfully exclaims*)
   Schaunard, our methods possibly may differ,
   But yet two kindly acts we'll do: (*pointing to the coat*)
   Mine's this one, and yours—leave them alone in there.
Sch.: (*overcome by emotion*) Philosopher, you're right!
   'Tis true; I'll go!
(*He looks about him: then, to justify his exit, he takes up the water bottle and goes out after Colline, gently closing the door. Mimi opens her eyes, and seeing that all have gone, holds out her hand to Rudolph, who affectionately kisses it*)
Mimi: Have they left us? (*Rudolph nods*)
   To sleep I only feigned,
   For I wanted to be alone with you, love.
   So many things there are that I would tell you.
   There is one, too, as spacious as the ocean,
   As the ocean, profound, without limit:
   You are my love, my all, and all my life!
(*putting her arms round Rudolph's neck*)

Rud.: Ah! Mimi! my pretty Mimi!

Mimi: (*letting her arms drop*) You still think I'm pretty!

Rud.: Fair as the dawn in Spring!

Mimi: No, the simile fits not; you meant to say:

Fair as the flame of sunset.

"They call me Mimi; (*like an echo*)

They call me Mimi, but I know not why."

Rud.: (*in tender, caressing tones*)

Back to her nest comes the swallow in Spring-tide.

(*He takes out the bonnet and gives it to Mimi*)

Mimi: (*gaily*) Why, that's my bonnet! (*motions* Rudolph *to put the bonnet on her head*)

Why, that's my bonnet!

(*makes* Rudolph *sit next to her, and rests her head on his breast*)

Ah! do you remember how we both went shopping

When first we fell in love?

Rud.: Yes, I remember.

Mimi: This room was all in darkness!

Rud.: While you, you were so frightened!

Then the key you mislaid, love.

Mimi: And to find it you went groping in the darkness.

Rud.: Yes, searching, searching.

Mimi: And you, my young master,

Now I can tell you frankly,

That you soon managed to find it.

Rud.: It was Fate that did help me.

Mimi: It was dark, and my blushes were unnoticed. (*faintly repeating Rudolph's words*)

"Your tiny hand is frozen,

Let me warm it into life!"

It was dark, and my hand then you clasped—

(*a sudden spasm half suffocates her; she sinks back fainting*)

Rud.: (*raising her in alarm*) Oh! God! Mimi!

(*At this moment Schaunard returns, and hearing Rudolph's exclamation, hastens to the bedside*)

Sch.: What now?

Mimi: (*opens her eyes and smilingly reassures Rudolph and Schaunard*)

Nothing; I'm better.

Rud.: (*gently lowering her*) Gently, for goodness' sake!

MIMI: Yes, forgive me: now it's over.

(MUSETTA *and* MARCEL *cautiously enter;* MUSETTA *carrying a muff, and her companion a phial*)

MUS.: (*to* RUDOLPH) Sleeping?

RUD.: (*approaching* MARCEL) Just resting.

MAR.: I have seen the doctor.

He'll come—I bade him hasten.

Here's the tonic.

(*Takes a spirit lamp, and placing it upon the table, lights it*)

MIMI: Who is it?

MUS.: I—Musetta. (*Approaches Mimi and gives her the muff. Helped by Musetta, she sits up in bed, and, with almost infantine glee, seizes the muff*)

MIMI: So soft it is and feathery!

No more will my poor fingers be frozen,

For this muff shall keep them warm. (*to* RUDOLPH)

Did you give me this present?

MUS.: (*eagerly*) Yes!

MIMI: You thoughtless fellow! Thank you.

It cost you dear. (RUDOLPH *bursts into tears*)

Weep not: I'm better.

Why should you weep for me?

Here love. . . ever with you! . . .

(*thrusts her hands into the muff; then she gradually grows drowsy, gracefully nodding her head, as one who is overcome by sleep*)

My hands are much warmer: now I will sleep!

(RUDOLPH, *reassured at seeing* MIMI *fall asleep, gently moves away from the bedside, and motioning the others not to make any noise, approaches* MARCEL)

RUD.: What said the doctor?

MAR.: He'll come.

MUS.: (*who is busily heating the medicine, brought by* MARCEL, *over the spirit-lamp, as she unconsciously murmurs a prayer*)

Oh! Mary! Blessed Virgin!

Save, of thy mercy, this poor maiden!

Save her, Madonna mine, from death!

(RUDOLPH, MARCEL *and Schaunard whisper together. Every now and then Rudolph goes on tiptoe to the bed, and then rejoins his companions. Musetta, interrupting, bids Marcel place a book upright on the table, so as to shade the lamp*)

Here there should be a shade,
Because the lamp is flickering!
Like this. (*resuming her prayer*)
And, oh! may she recover!
Madonna! holy mother! I merit not thy pardon,
But our little Mimi is an angel from Heaven!

(RUDOLPH *approaches* MUSETTA, *while* SCHAUNARD *goes on tiptoe to the bedside; with a sorrowful gesture he goes back to* MARCEL)

RUD.: I still have hope. Do you think it serious?

MUS.: Not serious.

SCH.: (*hoarsely*) Marcel, she is dead!

(*Marcel in his turn goes up to the bed, and retreats in alarm; a ray of sunshine falls through the window upon Mimi's face; Musetta points to her cloak, which, with a grateful glance, Rudolph takes, and standing upon a chair, endeavors to form a screen by stretching the cloak across the window-pane*)

COL.: (*quietly entering and putting some money on the table near Musetta*)
How is she?

RUD.: See, now! She's tranquil.

(RUDOLPH, *turning round, sees* MUSETTA, *who makes a sign to him that the medicine is ready; getting off the chair, he is suddenly aware of the strange demeanor of* MARCEL *and* SCHAUNARD)

RUD.: (*huskily, almost in a speaking voice*)
What's the meaning of this going and this coming,
And these glances so strange?

(*He glances from one to the other in consternation*)

MAR.: (*unable to bear up any longer, hastens to embrace* RUDOLPH *as he murmurs*) Poor fellow!

RUD.: (*flings himself on Mimi's bed, lifts her up, shakes her by the hand, and exclaims in tones of anguish*) Mimi! Mimi!

(*he falls, sobbing, upon her lifeless form*)

(*Terror-stricken*, MUSETTA *rushes to the bed, utters a piercing cry of grief; then kneels sobbing, at the foot of the bed*. SCHAUNARD, *overcome, sinks back into a chair; to the left*, COLLINE *stands at the foot of the bed, dazed at the suddenness of this catastrophe*. MARCEL, *sobbing, turns his back to the footlights. The curtain slowly falls*)

A Note About the Author

Giuseppe Giacosa (1847–1906) and Luigi Illica (1857–16 December 1919) were Italian librettists best known for collaborating on several operas. Giacosa was born near Turin and attended the local university where he studied law. Meanwhile, Illica grew up near Piacenza but eventually moved to Milan and became a journalist. Both men began their theatrical careers in the 1870s, which led to an imminent meeting. Together, they worked alongside Italian composer Giacomo Puccini to create some of his most notable operas including *La bohème*, *Tosca* and *Madama Butterfly*. All three are considered major figures in the world of performing arts.

A Note from the Publisher

Spanning many genres, from non-fiction essays to literature classics to children's books and lyric poetry, Mint Edition books showcase the master works of our time in a modern new package. The text is freshly typeset, is clean and easy to read, and features a new note about the author in each volume. Many books also include exclusive new introductory material. Every book boasts a striking new cover, which makes it as appropriate for collecting as it is for gift giving. Mint Edition books are only printed when a reader orders them, so natural resources are not wasted. We're proud that our books are never manufactured in excess and exist only in the exact quantity they need to be read and enjoyed.

bookfinity™

Discover more of your favorite classics with Bookfinity™.

- Track your reading with custom book lists.
- Get great book recommendations for your personalized Reader Type.
- Add reviews for your favorite books.
- AND MUCH MORE!

Visit **bookfinity.com** and take the fun Reader Type quiz to get started.

Enjoy our classic and modern companion pairings!

Classic & Modern